Santa Clara County Free Library

California

Alum Rock	Milpitas { Calaveras / Community Center / Sunnyhills	
Campbell		
Cupertino	Morgan Hill	
Gilroy	Saratoga { Quito / Village	
Los Altos { Main / Woodland	Stanford-Escondido	

Reference Center—Cupertino
For Bookmobile Service, request schedule

CONVERSATIONS WITH
KID COUGAR AND LIM HANG HIGH

Books by Joseph Faulds

Conversations with Kid Cougar and Lim Hang High

Have You Seen Jesus? A Trilogy in Prose and Poetry

Conversations with Kid Cougar and Lim Hang High

Joseph Faulds

An Exposition-Lochinvar Book

EXPOSITION PRESS   HICKSVILLE, NEW YORK

Most of the names used in these conversations
are fictitious substitutes

The photography is by Bruce Wagner of Dallas.

To Michelle

"The rich spoils of memories are mine."

—rancher's wife as she lay
on her deathbed

Introduction to Conversations

The rusticity is unlabored and natural. Kid Cougar and Lim Hang High are like two aged trees grown and weathered on the land they possess. The country style about these two is easy; the flavor reposes in their faces, body movements and speech; this quality is smoked and blended almost mystically in their personalities.

> By the black earth the ancient house
> is sustained as if it grew
> whole and entire from the founding
> sweet grassy land underneath.
>
> With this dwelling's fiber communes
> varied winds and elements,
> a benign quiet overhangs soft
> the overgrowth of near region.
>
> In the trees rising umbrella
> sheltering the old house live
> friendly squirrels and birds and bugs
> unbothered generations.
>
> A gray decrepit, sturdy home
> among fields sloping gently
> from patch to dark patch of chiggered
> woods undisturbed in fine peace.

Here is an aura of timelessness and age, weariness and strength. Yet somewhere within this serene, intrinsical permeation a hidden rhythm subtly lurks—a vigorous poetry full of high style and living/dying confidence like a sad but happy Jimmie Rodgers song.

The dogs alone seem immediately vital and fierce. These guardians of history run out from under the house snarling and barking, suggestive of field mice scattering from under a decayed stump when disturbed by men clearing a field.

Kid Cougar is shrewd; his shrewdness oozes from his Comanche wiseman eyes and wry horse trader's mouth. His midsection has an indefinable relaxed slouch. It is the belly of a cowboy who has straddled uncountable horses in an entire life span spent working with stock. If you look closely at the Kid you can see both the consoling peacemaker and the man who "won't back down for nothin'."

Lim Hang High is a collector's item. He is a philosopher-priest, gesturing nobly. He's an old vaudevillian dancer, and a gentle poet. Lim is a dignitarian lingering over from a day in American civilization that saw its dusk turn twilight fully a generation ago. He is an ancient man who wants a cane with a silver handle.

Kid Cougar and Lim Hang High are old men with grand hearts and rich memories. They value ideals, virtue and friendship. They revere God and hold in high esteem their fathers' faith. They are mischievous, old cowboys who can still remember gunplay, territory badmen, and rough humor, and who recall with satisfaction the idyllic sweethearts that they didn't marry. These two brothers are wise men whose wisdom rests cradled in a cumulative experience that will disappear with the high noon of modern civilization. For this reason I regard the preservation of the following conversations as something good and necessary.

Our culture grew from many roots. Herein may be found the primal distillation thereof, a remaining trace of an essence of the American Aeneid.

Memories

KID COUGAR: I'z born thuh 19th of November when thuh world wuz pretty young . . . I drawed mah manhood mighty slow . . . I used tuh play in thuh orchard, fish in thuh pool. When I got up around six years old, why, Dad he'd send me to thuh field with uh team uh horses. I'd bring out uh load of cotton—two thousand pound of cotton . . .

One uv these horses wuz uh old bay horse, blood bay, other'n wuz uh dapple iron gray, a four-year-old horse, that dapple iron gray horse—he run at thuh drop of uh hat . . . I don't see what kept 'em frum running away with me. I'z too small to handl' 'em. I'z too little to get thuh breast yoke up.

He'd always be a'shavin' while I wuz goin' after thuh cotton.

JOSEPH: Your Dad would be shaving?

KID: Yow, he'd always shave for he'd go to thuh gin.

JOSEPH: Use a straight razor?

KID: Yow—an old straight razor—when he went tuh town he'd always buy cheese an' crackers, an' I always looked forward tuh him come'n in with those cheese an' crackers.

JOSEPH: Sure . . .

KID: That wuz uh treat to us you see.

JOSEPH: Yes . . .

KID: But we had everything tuh eat—meat, all kinds uv beans.

JOSEPH: Raised your own hogs, didn't you?

KID: We'd kill four er five big hogs ever winter . . . he'd always make it in after dark ever night. I don't know what he done when he got tuh town, but don't make any difference how early he got started in thuh morning, it wuz always ten o'clock when he got in every night, but he drove his team along, and it'd be just as dark as smallpox.

JOSEPH: What kind of roads were there then, Kid?

KID: Just old dirt roads—they wuzn't a highway a-thought of . . .

KID: There's some old quiltin' frames out here on thuh back porch that mother used to use quiltin' on 'em . . . and I think there's four of 'em, they're about eight b' tens—it'd take her thirty days to quilt one uv them quilts.

JOSEPH: The quilts were of good quality though, weren't they?

KID: Oh yeah, we got—I guess there's fifty here in this ol' quilt box, I guess there's up around fifty that has never been on thuh bed.

JOSEPH: Really?

KID: Now you talk about keen quilts, boy they're keen . . . there's no tellin' how many there is up aroun' thuh back room—prob'ly forty er fifty. But she said "I want to quilt you boys enough quilts to have enough to cover up with as long as you live"—well the cover's goin' tuh outlast us. She was uh keen hand . . . she was uh good hand tuh render lard, we'd kill hogs . . .

JOSEPH: Lard from the hogs?

KID: Took that fat yuh see out uv that meat. It wuz always my turn after I got up any size to cut thuh meat up, cut up thuh sausage, grind thuh sausage—we'd put it in five gallon jars— thuh sausage.

JOSEPH: Did you have an old smokehouse?

KID: Yeah—we had uh smokehouse, uh meat box—we'd smoke that meat right dark brown, washed it with cold water—warm water'd run the salt in on it . . . Dig uh little trench out there, build your fire up out uv green pecans . . .

JOSEPH: Green pecans?

KID: Green pecans is as good as hickory.

JOSEPH: The pecan leaves or the pecan wood?

KID: Pecan wood, green pecan wood, it is second-growth stuff

. . . you know, Joe, second-growth pecan is just as good as hickory. Are you comin' all right, Lim? [*Lim Hang High enters den*]

KID: Oh, ah started in a-ridin', Joe, when I wuz uh pretty young boy, jist uh little o' kid, an' I'd get in a wrangle with horses . . . they'd throw me.

JOSEPH: Bet you've been kicked around a few times . . .

KID: Yeah, I've been broke, both arms, nose broke, kicked uh good many times. But I've been kicked thirty feet before.

JOSEPH: No kidding?

KID: Shore have . . . but tuh you take uh feller gettin' kicked that away, well that'll soon quit being funny.

JOSEPH: It will, won't it.

KID: Yeah . . . will for uh fact, I remember one time, ol' Lim rolled a wheel barrow up behind that old bay horse, he spooked an throwed me off an broke my arm and they never did take me to th Doctor at all . . . they jist pulled my arm up here [*Kid gestures*] an' put it in a sling; but you know Mother 'ud take it out of that sling an' straighten it out ever day—keep it from bein' stiff . . .

JOSEPH: Right . . .

KID: She put wet clay, yeller clay up the fingers, an' kept that around my arm . . . an' I wore that thang, it seemed tuh me like two months . . . two months time it got well, ah got mah leg broke.

JOSEPH: How'd you do that one, Kid?

KID: Horse . . . I'z always into somethin' with horses . . . and I remember one time Dad got uh iron gray mare out uv Amarillo, he's always buyin' stock yuh know, by thuh carload, bringin' it home . . .

JOSEPH: Yes?

KID: Brought that mare in, and had uh old bay mare with uh big ol' long-legged bay colt, you couldn't lead this bay mare —she's spooky, never had been handled.

JOSEPH: Right. [*Dog begins to bark intermittently*]

KID: An' I led this bay mare, an' this ol' bay colt, he's foll'in along behind. I jus' took 'em up thuh way en' got 'em uh drink of water . . . I started back to thuh barn with 'em, and ah's—oh, I don' know . . . ah's about five years old.

JOSEPH: Five years old?

KID: This ol' colt, he got behind his mammy, a good many feet, he cum uh loopin' down through there in uh run, an' he started tuh jump over me. Instead of jumpin' over me, why he hit me in back of thuh head with his knees, and it stuck mah head in thuh ground up to muh shoulders.

JOSEPH: To the shoulders?

KID: An' it mashed muh mouth an' skinned my nose, kinda got me bunged up pretty bad . . . but thuh last time ah got broke up I'z uh pretty good-sized boy, 'bout seventeen years old.

JOSEPH: Seventeen?

KID: And I remember there's some people lived over on top of thuh hill here that wuz named Franklin, John Franklin an' his wife; it was up in thuh evening I'd say about three o'clock . . .

JOSEPH: Three o'clock in the afternoon?

KID: Yeah . . . I told John, I said, "My arm's broke." He said, "No, it's not." Then along late in thuh evening, why I went ahead and eat supper with my left arm broke and I say, "Yes, it is broke." He says, "I'll take you over tuh Mr. Baken."

JOSEPH: Was the arm swelled up pretty badly?

KID: Yes, we walked across thuh creek over there, and it (the arm) had begun to get swelled an' red . . . Mr. Baken said, "Yeah, his arm's broke." He said, "well, let's go back tuh thuh house an' I'll saddle up uh couple of horses and we'll go to thuh doctor." . . . (we) went up there tuh Doc Jones, he (Doc) had uh couple uv boys a little bit younger than I wuz, and he sent 'em out to thuh smokehouse after'n old apple box. They went in thuh smokehouse an' got 'n old apple box . . . Doc got thuh apple box an' cut thuh splints, he put 'em on that arm—he got 'em down pretty tight . . . next morning, boy—that ol' arm wuz swelled up tight . . . I told Dad, "ah, you saddle up uh horse—I'm going back up there un see if he ain't got mah arm bound too tight" . . .

well he got me uh horse saddled up and I got on him, rode over . . . I told him "Doc, I b'lieve you got mah arm bound up too tight." He chewed tobaccer all thuh time; he said, "No! it's not bound up too tight unless it turns blue." He said, "if it goes to turnin' blue—come back now un I'll slack it off a little bit . . ."

JOSEPH: If it turns blue, it's too tight . . .

KID: Yeah . . . I wore that thing six weeks on mah arm an' they's gonna have entertainment up here at Indian Creek— I wanted to change shirts, change underwear . . .

JOSEPH: For the party?

KID: Had tuh cut mah underwear off me, couldn't bring that over that muh splint . . . well he says, "I'll tell you what I'll do, I'll take that splint off your arm, if you'll keep it in a sling all the time with uh piece of cardboard . . ." he said, "don't be a-ridin' uh horse." Well, I didn't tell him what I'z gonna do, I'z gonna ride uh horse (chuckles delightedly and I laugh).

JOSEPH: And go dancing!

KID: He took thuh splint off my arm, I changed clothes that night—got on 'n old black stag horse . . . got uh . . . swingin' pace . . . I rode that old horse up there tuh that entertainment that evening. I passed uh fellah's place that had uh big ol' brindle bulldog and he (the bulldog) shore did like to run uh horse. That dog he cut in after me; I think, "Well, I'll jist outrun you." I kicked that ol' horse out and I outrun thuh dog. Now what if thuh horse 'ud fell with me with that broke arm? . . . broke it again.

JOSEPH: You might have compounded it.

KID: Oh I use to, I'z always doing the unusual. I don't see how I'h ever got grown.

JOSEPH: Kid, it is true or false that horse color affects temperament?

KID: Huh-uh—don't have uh thing in thuh world tah do with disposition of your horse.

JOSEPH: I wouldn't think so.

KID: Now, they usetah say that uh yellah horse—they called them claybanks, these old-timers. But where they had a black stripe down their back and around their legs and acrost their withers they said he was uh hard-twisted horse. But I've saw some yellow horses that was very mean, I rode some that wuz pretty ugly. But you take a blue horse with black casting across his withers an' up an' down his back un behind his legs—he's uh tough horse too, they had lots of them in Oklahoma. But we'z in Oklahoma a-horse hunting. You see there usetah be lots uv them back in thuh mountains, east uv Stringtown. We went in there, we's gonna high-horse a bunch uh horses. In uh full moon, you know, why you can just start 'em a-movin'. Don't let 'em stop for water nor grass. Just keep 'em a-movin' all the time. When they first start they'll start in uh run. But you'll have tuh use horses for relay. You can't ride thuh same horse all thuh time, you'll ride 'em to death.

JOSEPH: Right.

KID: So just keep 'em a-movin' all day an' all night. It'll take yuh about forty-eight hours to run 'em down. But when you get about forty-eight hours, why, you'll begin to slow down. They'll be down by uh walk.

JOSEPH: Right.

KID: But where you go tuh ropin' that way, wh' you've got to have several riders, take care of these horses yuh rope. Yuh cant tie 'em up—they'll go tuh fightin' thuh rope, you see, and some of 'em 'll break their legs.

JOSEPH: Sure. Wild horses will fight until they do hurt themselves, won't they?

KID: Uh-huh (yes). But you can get 'em out in thuh open. Thuh best way is to get 'em out in thuh open somewhere where they can't get into uh fence or into any timber, or go off uh cliff with ye. Jist git on 'em an' ride 'em. But they're rough . . . but you take them wild horses that away, Joe, you can ride 'em three or four times—course now he'll just be green broke.

JOSEPH: Right.

KID: Won't be bridle-wise. But you'll have him pretty well broke. Now you can't hardly catch one out in thuh open a-tall.

JOSEPH: The more you ride one the better he'll handle, right?

KID: They'll get down pretty tame, but they won't never git gentled. You got to watch one all thuh time.

JOSEPH: You mean if a horse grows into maturity wild he will never be as dependable as one raised in domestication?

KID: I remember one time I went to uh fellah's place an' he had some horses out uv the mountains uv New Mexico. Brought three yellers an' one gray—he wadn't a dapple iron gray, he'z jus' gray. I had'n old ropin' that I wuz tryin' to peddle for all thuh four uv these ponies—they jus' pony horses 'bout seven and uh half. But you couldn't get in a hunnerd yards of them things unless you ride up on 'em. But you take jist a feller a-walkin up, why you couldn't get near 'em. They uz jest as spooky as they could be. But you take all them horses out of the West, Joe, they're different-natured horses from what we raise here. They've always got that spook in 'em. An' you cain't trust none of 'em. You know these horses raised in here, why they're dependable. But you can just depend on them like you can a person. But you take them western horses—just the least little thing they'll jist go up jist like uh firecracker. You cain't trust them range horses.

JOSEPH: The ones that grew up out on the range.

KID: If you ever run out uv water out there in them deserts, Joe, turn your burros loose. They'll waller, an' stand around a while. But if there's water in wind distance, they'll find it. The closer they get to, the faster they'll go. They may not be but uh washpan of it, but they can smell it. There's some uv that water out there that's poison. Got natural "strichnyne" in it.

JOSEPH: Strychnine?

KID: If yuh drink it, it'll kill yuh, boy. If a horse wuz raised in that country an' he hit thuh water with his nose, don't drink it. If he won't drink it, don't you drink it.

KID: Dad, he wuz uh medium stature feller, and he wuz a right smart of uh whiz-bang hisself—he wuz uh wrassler . . . an he wuz the stoutest little man I ever saw—'bout uh hunnerd

an' fordy-five pounds back when I wuz uh kid wuz as heavy
as he ever got . . . He wuz five feet an' ten inches tall . . .
We usetah go a-huntin' with a little o' black n' white spaniel
dog. An' we'd jump uh squirrel. He'd run the squirrel, the
dog 'ud run Dad, an' I'd run the dog. He'd outrun uh dog
an' run that squirrel in uh creek bank, he'd grab 'im up uh sharp
post an' he'd commence tuh diggin' him out; I'd say "Now
wait Dad till I kina catch my breath." "Ah hell! Let's dig
'im out while he's tired 'n ketch 'im." An he'd jist git up an'
outrun that squirrel an' run all over him an' step on 'im.

As a young man he roamed a territory seeking adventure.
He carried a gun and used it. Later, he married and became a
family man. He was a natural musician and sang in the church
choir at "Sunday go to meetin' " gatherings.

KID: His mother died when he uz twelve years old. An' he'd
       git on his horse an' go after the doctor of uh night. An' I fergit
       that old doctor's name. An' this ol' doctor, he'd saddle his
       horse an' never cinch the saddle. He'd ride in uh lope an'
       Dad said he'd run the ol' doctor.

When he was a child his uncle came visiting, bringing fresh-
killed deer draped over the withers of a spotted horse. The
spotted horse was wiry, small and tough. The uncle was neither
tall nor short; his shoulders were not broad but his chest was
like a barrel and his bare legs were inordinately muscled;
his hair was long and black and an eagle feather hung from
one side of his head. When he spoke, the child could not
understand, but when he roughly tousled the boy's hair and
smiled at him it seemed that they two shared a private joke, and
he took the boy for rides, holding him on the withers of the
spotted horse, which leaped through the woods at breakneck
speed, jumping creek beds and running up hills which the sun
illumined red before the shadows came. The fleet little horse
would sweat, and the sweat lightly scalded the child's skin. The
warrior sometimes laughed when he saw squirrels playing in the

trees and spoke again in that musical tongue which the child did not comprehend.

Many years later on a trail drive, the cowboys were approached by two warriors and a young woman. The two men were the last of a soldier band who had refused the degradation of the concentration camp called "reservation." These two warriors and their now dead comrades were responsible for a large number of white soldiers making the "noble sacrifice." The cowboys did not want a fight. Quickly they cut out the worst calf of the herd and sent it running toward the warriors who sat quietly on their horses at a small distance. The older of the two warriors wore in his long grey hair an eagle feather. There was a mixed-blood cowboy riding drag who was feared for his capability with the forty-five which rested lightly in its holster. A look of recognition passed between these two and over the old warrior's impassive mask of a countenance a faint smile momentarily spread. Later when the mixed-blood cowboy heard of the grey-haired warrior's death, something seemed to die in his cowboy heart, heretofore carefree.

KID: Yuh float with yer mount, yuh see, yuh jist, well yer jist light as uh feather on yer mount's back. If yuh rare back yuh see why that tars yer animal. Or if yuh look back while yer ridin' yuh know first one way then another, that'll tar yer animal. Jist float with yer mount. Jist be uh part of 'em, why yer all right.

KID: It's been uh good many moons, Joe. I wish you could uh met Uncle Bert.

Two uncles of my friends once broke jail in Donahn. They were being held in relation to a gunfight which had not been conducted quite properly. The two brothers were sharpening a butcher knife and a third man was speaking with them. Suddenly a violent argument broke out between one brother and the third party. Their uncle took off his gun belt and offered to fight the man. "Take off yuh're guns an' ah'll whup yuh!" The man waited until he thought their uncle was dropping his belt and then drew one of his own guns and fired. Their uncle had kept hold of the end of his gun belt, however, and leaped behind a tree while recovering his pistols. The bullet fired at the uncle struck the tree and an instant later he fired and mortally wounded the unscrupulous gunman. The other uncle was enraged at this attempt to kill his brother by foul play and, taking the now razor-sharp butcher knife in hand, he jumped on the dying man and cut him in two, from the right shoulder to the waist, taking off all the ribs on that side of his chest.

KID: Old Doc Bowler said they couldn't get bodies in the medical school. There'd come a bad night when it's stormin', rainin', thunderin' an' lightnin', they'd hitch up a team to uh wagon, put uh sheet o'vr it an' go to uh cemetery, dig up uh body an' bring it in. An' they had uh little ol' cot, in this wagon, yuh know, they'd lay this body on this cot. An' said they alwuz took 'em uh quart uh whisky with 'em, so they could drink, yuh know, comin' back. Said when they'd start tuh take uh drink they'd always hold this quart out tuh this corpse, say, "Want uh drink, stiff?" Said one night the ol' boy he slipped in this cot yuh know under this sheet, an' put this body in under the cot. Said they's drivin' along in the wagon said they all started to take uh drink said they held the bottle out to this corpse yuh know, and said, "Yu‑onta drink, stiff?" Sez this ol' boy he commenced tuh movin' aroun' under thuh sheets said, "B'lieve ah will!" (Kid laughs) Said, man they's uh bunch uh them piled outa that wagon, they had the wagon loaded with students. Said they jist scattered everywhere, said they like tuh never got 'um all gathered up! I don't thank there's but two knew this fellah'uz on this cot yuh know, covered up with this sheet . . . But he (the body) 'ud have tuh be pretty fresh. Yuh see back then they didn't embalm anybody a-tall. Yuh know rigor mortis ud set in jest uh few 'ours. Put coins on the eyes. Two-bit pieces er fifty-cent pieces, push their eyes to lay them coins on 'em 'till they got cold. They didn't have any coolin' board tuh put 'em on. But I been tuh funerals Joe, when you couldn't hardly stay aroun' 'em a-tall.

The Kid knew a veterinarian who would not shake hands with people for fear of contamination.

KID: He got his fanger hung on a barbed wire an' he jabbed her pretty good. An' he wuz jist uh lookin' at it, talkin' about it an' ah said, "Why, Doc, I don't pay any attention tuh uh little scratch like that." He said, "Hell, I do," said "I've had blood pois'n three times!" But he'z thuh most pecul'ar fellah you ever saw. He wuz uh tooter. I think he eat some bad fish an' it killed 'im. But don't never eat tuna fish, Joe.

There was a man who was a member of three professions, or, if you will, two professions and a trade. This versatile fellow practiced surgery, dental surgery, and carpentry.

KID: He uz goin' tuh pull Boyd Long's suh tooth yuh know, he had uh toothache. Said he went down there said it uz jist hotter 'n hell 'ith thuh lid on, an' said he told doctor what he wanted, said there'z wagon settin' out. Said Doc said, "Ah! By God bet I'h pulled that wagon bed full there!" Said he got hold of it with uh fahceps, squeezed it too hard, took the crown off uv it. Said God, he never had anything tuh hurt him as bad in his life. But I'z never in a dentist's shop in my life, Joe.

KID: We'd eat in there in that bedroom—tha'z thuh kitchen then. Mother 'ud fry half-moon pies out uh homemade dried peaches. God, boy we had 'em. We had uh hunnerd an forty bearin' peach trees here. We raised all kinds uh fruits an' berries, grapes, an' raised cotton, 'n corn, 'n oats. I thought we could have some uh thuh worst crops I ever saw in my life. We'd try tuh get thuh cotton hoed out by the Lineville picnic. Sometimes we didn't make it. I'd go tuh thuh picnic horseback.

Kid says that if a man were looking for a wife-mate that he would drive a buggy with a narrow seat. It was much safer to remain horseback. Marriage, says the Kid, not only limits a man's social expression but also changes his character—usually for the worse.

KID: All kinds uh garden-truck, all kinds uh beans, pumpkins, squashes, sweet potaters, Irish potaters, yah-boy we raised ev'rything, plenty uh bees. But we'd have this dining room all across here stacked with honey—gallon buckets uh honey. When it's rainin' we'd bucket honey, out here'n this bee house.

Of all the broncs Kid Cougar ever rode, the roughest was a little mule out of West Texas. Kid once green-broke fourteen horses in one day. One should leave one's horses's mane long so that a six-shooter may be concealed therein, the hammer closed on a strand of hair in order to secure the gun in its place.

KID: I've rode some awful rough horses, but that little mule he'd uh weighed uh bout uh thousand pounds. I couldn't hear anything for three or four days (after the ride). But he could turn handsprings. I draw an' idea he wuz the feistiest thang yuh ever saw.
JOSEPH: Kid, do you remember a horse named Midnight?
KID: Yow, I'm well acquainted with Midnight.

A man with one eye and one ear would ride out into the arena and shout with glee, "Booger Red, ugliest man livin' er dead!"

KID: Old Booger Red he had to slip up on uh dipper to get him uh drink uh water. He uz the ugliest I ever saw. But he had one eye an' one ear off. But he wuz the ugliest critter that yuh ever saw in yer life! I rode with 'em. He had uh little nigger with 'em he called old nigger Willie. Willie rode uh little Jenny. He'z uh clown. Ol' Booger Red could ride uh streak uh greased lightnin' an' carry uh wildcat under each arm. He didn't have no stirrups on his saddle nur any stirrup leathers. Jist had the hull. But yuh wanta come out over them ol' boys (broncs) an' float. Yuh wanta lead 'em out uh thuh shoot uh half uh jump. If yuh get uh half uh jump behind yuh won't never catch up an' the first thang yuh know yuh jist got uh horse-fall. Stick yer head in the ground up to yer shoulders.

JOSEPH: When was the last time you saw Booger Red?

KID: It uz uh-about nineteen an' twelve er thirteen. But there usetah be uh Indian come in here, Indian Joe, he's out uh Oklahoma. You talk about yer fancy trick'ry an' fancy roper boy! He wuz it.

JOSEPH: When did you last see him?

KID: It uz about uh . . . 'twenty-six I b'lieve.

KID: You take lots uh them ol' horses, they's uh, gentle broncs. There's lots uh diff'rence in things now, in everything, Joe, than back then. But you rode hell for leather back then.

JOSEPH: Lim, of all the young women with whom you were acquainted, which one was the prettiest of all?

LIM: . . . Miss Marguerite Anderson. I b'lieved everything she said. Pulled the wool over mah eyes. She wuz pretty. She 'uz dark-haired 'bout the color uh your little sister. She wuz just uh prittiest size. She'z black-eyed, dark-eyed. Dark, real dark brown. She wuz light complected. Had the prittiest form you ever saw! Breasts as large [*he makes an eloquent, graphic gesture*] an' she wuz plump an' well built. They wore the dresses long then an' yuh couldn't tell too much about how she wuz shaped up on thuh bottom. You had tuh find out about that. She wuz uh smart girl. She was uh winsome little outfit. She'z about five-foot-eight. She wuz very practical, a very practical little lady.

JOSEPH: What do you miss most about the old days, Lim? What do you miss most that is gone?

LIM: What we miss thuh most in our life is them early-day friends . . . and our parents. The old boys that were early day Texas pioneers—I miss them a lot. I wuz very thoughtful with them old fellas.

Kid and Lim's great-grandfather slept in a hollow log and ate the parched corn which an old Indian gave him. The old Indian said, "Eat this and you will keep away hunger." Corn has been changed since then and is bigger in size but less nutritious in quality now than then, says Kid Cougar.

LIM: These women 'cided tuh carry 'em off, but it didn't work, didn't work. After they got gone, Uncle Bat's partner says tuh him, says, "Bat, wuz them nice women?" Ol' Bat, (Lim shakes head slowly with eyes closed and lips pursed to depict Bat's answer. We both laughed).

Kid Cougar went for swims in the Kiamichi River until a friend of his showed him a twelve-foot-long alligator gar caught from the same spot in which the Kid had been swimming.

Once evening Kid Cougar told of an unhappy romance. It seems that back in the twenties and thirties there took place in this area a fundamentalist religious movement to which the Kid refers as a "holiness revival." One of the preachers involved in this movement was a young woman then in her early twenties named Jani Katherine. Jani K. had grown up in the West Texas oil fields and in her teens made money by performing as a prostitute for the oil field roughnecks. She then converted and was preaching at the "holiness" meetings when the Kid first saw her. When she preached she usually told in detail of her fall into sin and subsequent regeneration, intending, I suppose, to inspire her listeners with hope in relation to their own struggles with their perhaps somewhat lesser vices. She was very attractive, and a man named Ed Smith fell in love with her. Ed was not particularly distinguished in any way, except by the size and shape of his nose. This nose was remarkably like unto a rather large squash vegetable. Ed did not have Cyrano's other accomplishments, so in order to impress Jani K. he stayed all night in the church building, ostensibly to pray and wait for a spiritual revelation. As the night went on those who watched with him got sleepy and went home. Ed continued in his vigil until he fell asleep on a church bench. Now it seems that Ed was a very heavy sleeper. Two ruffians came in the church before sunrise looking for Ed and, discovering him to be asleep, they did a shameful thing. They urinated in his ear and poured a pint of moonshine spirits down his throat. Ed awoke in a very disturbed and discomfited state, but soon began to feel exceedingly happy, if the word "happy" may be used in such an artificial context. Unfortunately, Jani K. was not impressed. She married another man and when that man died years later she married again, but still not poor Ed. Poor Ed Smith became a miser with a thick money belt and never married, living out his life like an existentialist who never makes the heroic commitment and never gains a hold in the absolute.

KID: They said when he come to, he wuz gloriously happy.

LIM: He said, "I b'lieve I'll go out and help him bring it in." Said, "What d' you mean?" And he said, "Ed Smith's nose."

KID: Jist uh great big o' hump on his face, bout like uh bulldog been rattlesnake-bit.

JOSEPH: I'll be darned.

Kid says that Jimmie Rodgers had a supernatural voice and that he knew a young cowboy long ago who sang very similarly.

There was a woman who sent a Bible to their father as he lay dying. She said, "Tell him that I will pray for him." He said, "Tell 'er that I'll do mah own prayin'." Their father received a mortal injury when, as an old man, he lost control of a team that had been frightened by a new motorized road grader. The wagon overturned and crushed him, but it took him two years to die.

KID: Dad used tuh live in Thurman back in thuh eighties, an' they pulled thuh street cars with uh mule . . .

Grace was a percheron gelding who wore a size six shoe. Kid says of Grace, "Thuh Lord never put better horseflesh in uh hide." Grace worked faithfully for the Kid and Lim for over ten years and received his retirement pasture at the age of sixteen. (Kid says that it is immoral to turn an old horse over to the glue and dog food makers.) Grace was killed at the age of twenty-seven by Rocky the mule, then a young beast just gaining his prime. Rocky was nineteen hands tall, and he rushed upon Grace as the great percheron, weakened by age, stood meditating by the bank of a creek. Rocky knocked Grace over the bank side and down into the creek bed. Grace fell about fifteen feet and mired in the muddy creek bottom where he hit. The fall injured Grace internally, and the stress of being pulled from the mud made the injuries mortal. As Grace lay dying he groaned low and soft. The Kid was saddened at this because Grace was the best natured horse that he had ever known. Rocky the mule was mean and treacherous until the day of his death.

Kid says that horses differ from one another as much as people differ among themselves. Some horses are more intelligent than others; some are more educated, formally or informally; some horses are fine natured and some are mean, but these latter are never so ugly and petty as mean people; some horses suffer from mental illness. Kid cautions me to always remember that a horse can stand only a little more than his rider and that a good horseman feeds and cares for his horse before seeing to his own needs. There is a difference between a wild horse and an outlaw horse: a wild horse will buck one off and run; an outlaw horse will buck one off and then turn to kill one.

Kid Cougar has ridden more miles horseback and shod more horses than may be counted, and he has roped cattle without number. He has taught more than one mean bull manners with a blacksnake, been shot twice, and slept out on mountain and plain, in deep woods and valley land. Lonely grassy meadows and many wooden rodeo bleachers have been his bed and a horse blanket his bed clothes. The cold did not bother him, and the rain washed him clean. The last time that he stayed in Dallas, passing through from a Fort Worth rodeo, he slept in a house in Oak Cliff and was awakened by the sound of the milkman's horse clomping down the street. The milkman's horse was very intelligent and knew which houses to stop before without the milkman's prompting him, says Cougar.

My friend Lim Hang High says that his philosophy of ethics may be summed up in these words, "The truth is proof; it belittles all lies." Both brothers tell me that in the old time a man's word was sacred. If he robbed banks but kept his word when he gave it, he was still a man, albeit a bad one. But if he broke once his word he was not a man. Even if he spoke as an angel and did the deeds of a god, he was nothing at all if he broke his word. The world has changed.

KID: She could run jest like uh sage hen. But she wuz good-lookin' and had uh pritty form.

One of the earliest memories of Kid Cougar is of cattle. The range was still open, and the cattle had to be chased from the yard around the house. Kid was two and his mother set him on the porch and told him to stay there until the milling cattle were run off from the premises. The cows frightened him, however, and he climbed down the steps and hid under the porch. Later that day he was caught climbing upside down up an elm tree. Lim says that when the Kid was a small child horseflies were a favorite snack.

KID: Dad an' Mother 'ud build us uh wickeeup out in the cotton patch. Spread uh quilt out an' we'd git in under that thang yuh know, out uh thuh chiggers.

LIM: Mother 'ud make Kid uh sandwich. An' set 'im up in the door on thuh top step. An' we had an' old ash-colored hen. An old mother hen, ash colored with uh grey neck. Kid ud be uh-sittin' there eatin' his sandwich, an here'd come that old hen take it away from 'im . . .

KID: You remember that old pecan tree Lim? It had great big pecans on it. But I wuz a little bitty toot an' there's an elm tree stood right north of it bout six er eight feet. Dad made him uh trough an' he nailed it tuh this pecan tree an' this elm tree tuh feed thuh ol' pair uh horses . . .

KID: Uncle Billy C. wuz uh fiddler. He set his chair up in thuh middle uh thuh bed . . . set up in thuh bed an' fiddle.

Uncle Billy C. buried his favorite traveling mare in his wife's best bed quilt, and he could fiddle drunk even better than sober. When he was angry with his wife for leaving him for a time in order that she might visit relatives in San Antonio, he would defecate on the best bed sheets. Uncle Billy C. was a Confederate veteran.

LIM: Ever man that rode uh horse carried saddle bags. The makin's fer thuh tobaccah carried in thuh saddle bags. Dad wore two six-shooters, ball an' cap six-shooters, he told me one cold, cloudy, misty evenin' it got too cold for us in the cotton field.

JOSEPH: Did you carry two pistols when you rode with the cattlemen?

LIM: Yes, ah did. I had two good ones.

When Model T's became common young men from town sometimes drove out on Sundays to court country girls. Lim was out riding down a dirt road one afternoon when he was passed by just such a couple in a souped-up Model T. The young lady waved to Lim as the car raced past. Lim spurred his horse and overtook the car. As he passed on his running horse he leaned over from the saddle and patted the pretty maiden on the cheek. The speeding Model T was left in the dust trail of horse and horseman, and the young lady did not marry her town-bred suitor.

LIM: Well, when we crossed the other bridge—that wuz the funniest thing I ever saw—my horse's back feet hit uh loose plank. Mr. Moore wuz right behin' me. Well, when that plank flew up, it hit Mr. Moore's horse in the stomach! Between his legs yuh know, jus' smacked him good. Well, that scared Mr. Moore's horse an' he just went sideways, jumped right off at the en' uv the bridge. I looked back, Mr. Moore wuz uh come crawlin' out uh the ditch on his horse, his hat was jus' chugged down (we laugh) over his face. Shore did tickle me! (again we laugh) It uz uh hot Sundie mornin' in September.

Lim Hang High told me one night of an incident which may be sociologically monumental. It represents symbolically, I think, the last showdown between the old days of Kid and Lim and their fathers and the modern world.

Several young men, not of the country people, were joy riding down the maze of dirt roads and trails which lead to the back-country farms and ranches hereabouts. The speeding car suddenly came around the bend in the dirt trail that passes the old house in which my two ancient ghosts of history reside. The dogs were out running wolves in the brush, and Lim was caught unprepared on the side porch. Six young men with guns got out of the car and said vile things. They walked toward the porch where Lim stood his ground with a chopping axe that he had picked up from a stack of tools. Each of the six young men carried a rifle or a shotgun. A door from the house to the side porch opened and Kid Cougar stepped out. He walked down the steps and stood by the old well which is the only source of drinking water for the house. He held in his right hand his old single action forty-five. It was made in 1872, and he keeps it well oiled. The leader of the pack raised his rifle toward Kid and threatened to kill both the old cowboys. The Kid stuck his forty-five in his belt, cocking it as he did so. Then he said, "I draw an idea you jist ought uh git in yuh're vehicle an' git gone, boy." The young men stopped walking and looked at the old man, now not thirty feet away. There was a moment's pause as the Kid's eyes narrowed, and the armed moderns hesitated. Something about this old man with an old forty-five scared them. They began to back away slowly at first and then started to run as the dogs came crashing through the brush howling like Baskervillian fiends. By the time the dogs had reached the side porch, however, the late model car was speeding away and bumping badly over the dirt trail. I asked Lim if he had been worried about the possible outcome of this potential shootout. He said, "I shore wuz, boy! When I saw Kid pull back thuh hammer on his pistol I'z wonderin' what we uz goin' to do with all them six dead fellahs."

The boy was twelve years old and being the oldest male was entrusted with the grain for the mill. The Union soldiers stopped him and took the grain from the wagon and poured it out on the ground, laughing. The boy cried then, but two years later he got his desired revenge.

LIM: The Union soldiers had thuh town captive, yuh see, and they had pickets all aroun' thuh town.

The boy stole a valuable running horse from a Union officer. He bluffed his way through two picket lines and spurred the horse forward when ordered to dismount at a third picket. He was pursued hotly until in a dead run he jumped the horse across a chasm above a wide river. Some Dutch women down below washing in the river saw the great leap and cried out, "Look you! Look you at that boy!" The Yankee horsemen stopped at the edge of the chasm and fired their guns, but the horse and rider were very soon out of range.

LIM: He rode through that woods an' that timber an' he got lost. It got dark. Well, he decided he didn' know what tuh do he wouldn' do anythang at all. He got down off thuh horse, pulled thuh saddle off, made uh bed out uh thuh blanket. Said when he laid on thuh groun', laid there awhile said he heard bells . . . He got up an' he could see thuh campfire. There were two wagons an' they'z aroun' thuh campfire an' they'z a-cookin' supper.

When one cowboy nodded asleep in the saddle on a night ride the other cowboy would spur the sleeping man's horse and watch while the rudely awakened fellow rode his pitching mount back down. Then the awakened cowboy would try to catch the prankster in order to "whip 'im."

KID: Uncle John had uh mare. Said she uz gentle. Said he had an' ol' muzzle loadin' squirrel rifle. Said he had that ol' squirrel rifle. Said he had that ol' squirrel rifle an' uh old dollar watch. Said there's uh ranchman, horse ranchman right close. Said they went over an' said he held up this ol' horse ranchman, yuh know, tuh swap 'em this rifle an' th' watch fer uh horse.

The Klu Klux Klan in the post-Civil-War days was made up of Confederate diehards, says Kid. They wore white sheets in an attempt to make the uneducated former slaves believe that the ghosts of fallen Confederate soldiers were haunting the nights. The revived KKK of the nineteen twenties and thirties was composed of "drunkards, thugs an' whoremongers," says Kid. Lim investigated the KKK in the twenties by pretending to be interested in joining the evil group. He was not allowed to wear his guns to meetings so he carried a throwing knife under his shirt in a shoulder sheath. The leader of these thugs, Lim tells me, used to get drunk and turn over his cotton hauling truck regularly. Lim says that he and the Kid know an old black man who is the last of the old-time Texas muleskinners. The oldest grave in the family cemetery is the grave of a slave.

Kid Cougar got his name when as a young man he faced down a hungry mother cougar. Kid was unarmed at the time and ran the cougar off by throwing rocks at her.

KID: But you take back in pioneer days fellah's comin' in from the west there in Fenton, if he didn't get in before dark he stopped. Camped yuh know somewhere. He didn' come through there after dark. It wuz certain if yuh come through there they'd drop ye.

JOSEPH: Robbers?

KID: Yah-boy!

A man was murdered in his wife's sight and buried with the toes of his boots sticking out of the ground. His murderers were hung, but for years the boot toes were visible to passers-by.

When a wagon train was held up one day, the robbers searched everyone but a twelve-year-old boy. This boy had all the money concealed in his clothing.

Kid Cougar's best friend was killed by Friday the Thirteenth. Jack Smith was a Choctaw and a great bronc rider. When he rode a bronc in the rodeo, Jack never used a pick-up man. He would leap off the horse at the finish of a ride and land on his feet. One evening he rode Friday the Thirteenth successfully and made his leaping dismount. Friday sunfished and kicked Jack in the stomach with both hind feet just as the cowboy landed standing on the arena ground. Jack was dead when the Kid reached him moments later.

The old men tell me that there was a time when the land was virgin, for the original peoples respected the earth. A man could easily find his supper on the ground in the woods. Indian medicine was derived from herbs and roots and was very effective. Then the European invaders came and raped the land and brought horrid diseases such as smallpox and cholera, diseases for which the Indian had no medicine.

LIM: That wuz ol' Geronimo's warriors . . . Apache.

KID: One uh thuh boys said, "B'lieve they got ol' Tom." One uh thuh other boys said, "No, they didn't either. Here he comes jist a-runnin' like hell!" (on horseback) But he outrun 'em." Said he'z ridin' uh good "nag." He didn' call 'um uh "horse." Called 'em uh "nag." Said he'z ridin' uh good "nag." But they got his partners.

JOSEPH: Now in most movies when cowboys and Indians fight over something, the cowboys are shown shooting the Indians, not running from them.

KID: Well, they run.

Kid says that the preferred way of fighting Indians in the old days was to greatly outnumber the Indians or attack them during a truce while talking peace with their leaders.

KID: But they'd go back there with uh twenty foot pair uh schooners (wagons) an' they'd get uh few barrels uv mollassees, uh barrel er two uh whisky, side meat n' beans. Uh little bit uh sugar if they could find it, brown sugar. Caps fer guns, yuh know, old muzzle loadin' guns . . .

Cougar showed me a cascading waterfall. From the top of the fall into the water pool at the bottom fell a twice-wounded gunman, hunted down and shot the second time as he rested, wounded after an unsuccessful and disastrous attack on a ranch house.

The creaking wooden merry-go-round swung slowly about as the old mule pulled forward following his dusty circular path. A young couple rode in the outer seats and smiled gently at each other. In the inner seat rode a minstrel picking a guitar and singing a simple song about a rat . . .

The last barn dance took place in forty-three at the north barn. Faded names are written in the tack room where Kid Cougar fiddled and Lim Hang High picked the mandolin as the couples danced up and down the dirt-floor hall. Cobwebs float where people laughed and limp piles of decrepit old harness rests on pegs. Ancient tack lies about the barn in an attitude of emptied Buddhist resignation. The ghosts of many horses and the spirits of mules occupy the dark recesses of stall and chute. The sundown breeze kisses the rotting fiber of weathered wood and makes the old barn sigh with a light nostalgic moan. The words of a song touch my fancy.

I'm getting so old and feeble, and my days are nearly
done.
Oh, how I long for the prairie where the cattle and
mustangs run.
Take me out there where the cowboys sing in the
campfire's gleam.
Oh, let me rest out in Texas, the land of my boyhood
dreams.

As I drive down country highways, gravel rock roads, and
dirt trails in late night I sometimes feel as if I am going where
I've been but can never go again except in the depths of my
distant, yet near, memories. I see once again certain things
which no longer are evident anywhere but in me. Simple time
passage and change do not jolt the mind, but the death of beauty
and the passing away of great souls and the present remoteness
of a once vivid and intimately familiar life form are paradox
and intensely odd. Transcendental fall afternoons, cool, wet spring
mornings, bitter winter nights, summer white heat, a brave deed,
a soft light, an emotion, a certain quiet conversation, and a
smile that is a simple smile and nothing else. Here someone
died, a child ran in the grass, an animal breathed, and rain
made dirt into mud. Struggle, violence, peace, earth, spirit, blood,
a falling star.

A youth
in the early nineteenth century left his home
an island place washed in the sea off the coast of
Ireland

He sailed to the continent of bloodsoaked Europe
he sought adventure and fortune as he wandered
from state to state casting his fate to time and chance

In Germany he found grave trouble
over politics or religion or women or perhaps
hungry he stole a loaf of bread thinking he might repay
someday

Now he stowed away on a ship with many sails
a hunted man seeking to save his life by hiding among
    the great waves
but soon he was discovered by the ship's company
maybe some one-eyed mate
caught the youth in the bilge giving up
his stolen bread
convulsively

Put to work an apprentice seaman the dreamer youth
on the ship of many sails sailed around the tip
of South America through many waters past many islands
    where other youths,
brown-skinned sons dreamed like he
of adventure

When the great ship reached the long shoreline of
    California, the youth
now weathered by wind, salt and sea water threw himself
    into the foam
swimming to the rocks where welcoming sea birds sat
    nesting in the sun
he staggered about until his land legs returned and then
he set out, clothed in sea soaked rags, walking quickly
    eastward
perhaps to avoid that one-eyed mate who came ashore in
    in a ship's boat
looking

On wandering the youth came to a bleached mission where
bells tolled and dedicated Spanish priests had taught gentle
    Indians
to accept the murdering yoke of Spain and to be forgiving
    Christians

A kind priest clothed and fed the maturing youth and he
    sat in mass
where a landowner's daughter loved his dreaming blue

Kid Cougar

Lim Hang High

Kid and Lim lighting up

Lim, Joseph and Kid

eyes and he too loved her
for her dark and burning but
demurring glance

The proud landowner presently sent his fiery sons,
lean horsemen to kill the youth and once again
the island man the dreaming child fled from his pursuers
into a sea of waves but now waves of sand
and burned by the sun the dreaming man uncannily
    survived
perhaps by drinking cactus milk and eating raw lizards

The blue-eyed man now set his eyes on the rising sun
and helped along the way by friendly men black haired
    men
kind Indians who had yet to learn that all the whites like
    Spanish men
brought death with their greed their dreaming eyes their
    ancient sins
sicknesses
and treachery

Many days in many majestic lays of land and
through many valleys, deserts and plains
and foothills of great mountains he walked without a
    horse except once
maybe he had a mare
briefly for he lost her in the night to a roaming
stallion

The blue-eyed man sparely bearded for he was fair
skinned and young grew leathery as he wandered quavering
    north
then south but always eastward eating abundant game
moving toward that sunrising which he began to love
for it seemed an old friend always beckoning in the
    morning
red

He came to Texas a state of Mexico and in the woods
among the dry and sweetened woods he came upon
a hoary woodsman kneeling over a fresh killed deer and
    scooping
in the cup of eager hands blood from the deer's cut throat
and drinking lapping the warm blood which for its part
protested by running down from his toothy mouth staining
    his grizzled
grey beard
the wandering man the island man went to the woodman's
    home where
no longer wore he rags but buckskins like the woodsman
    and he worked in the field and hunted the deer and
    cared for the woodman's herd then
after a season and a little while he married the woodman's
    daughter
she was fair her hair hung soft she loved the blue-eyed
    island man
and they were happy in those greening woods
together

A war came for Texas declared independence
and Santa Anna came with many brave soldiers from
    Mexico
to stop the historic succession but Santa Anna lost
his army failed and among the Texans who fought el
    presidente
at San Jacinto was the island man who received for his
    service a grant
of land not far from his home with the woodman's pretty
    daughter

On this land the island man whose clear blue eyes had
    beheld
such varied adventure and his young woman wife his
    lovely daughter of nature
lived and loved and grew their foods and cared for the
    herd
horses and cattle

To this man and his wife born were five young sons
men of the horse who rode together and when another
   war
the great Civil War came and Texas succeeded once again
five brothers strong horsemen brothers rode five fierce
   horses
eastward to the sound of cannon

KID: Grandad said he wore leather britches during thuh Civil
War. He said i'd rain, be rill cold, an' freeze.

JOSEPH: Yes . . .

KID: He said them ol' leather britches at night when he'd pull
'em off—I don't know what kind-uh sleepin' quarters he had—
said they'd freeze. Said he'd have tuh get up on thuh log next
mornin' to git his britches on.

JOSEPH: That must have been a curious sight.

KID: But he said one time they got in tah uh fight, un said he uz
runnin' a two year old roan filly un said sh's jist green broke.
They's retreatin', an' there wuzn't hardly any bridges at all.
He got on this filly an' kicked her out an' run up tuh this
swingin' bridge. An' said when she got t'at bridge she jist set
her feet an' come to a slidin' halt. Said he had uh rawhide
lariat an' when he come off her he jist pitched the loop
'round her neck. Started runnin', said she put right in after
'm. He said if she had'n a'followed him he uz gonna shoot
her down—didn't want thuh northern soldiers to git her.

JOSEPH: Right . . .

KID: Said he wuz the first fellah in thuh brush, runnin' an'
leadin' that retreat. [*The cocks are crowing*]
   Uncle Dick wuz the one that wuz sech a card in battle.
Said they'd always count ever fifth man out for a horse-holder.
Four 'ud fight an' one would hold thuh horses. Said Uncle
Dick when they got in-tah battle when thuh fight uz over, said
maybe he'd be uh half uh mile from 'um all with the horses.
Said he'd come up to Uncle Dick where he's at, say "What
the hell are yuh doin' down here, Dick?" "Oh dammit, Dink,
I thought if y'all got whupped I'd just be this fur on the way
with thuh horses." But he said Uncle Dick ud get in uh battle

an' jist git as sick as uh bird, jist puke jus' like a bird. Said one time the'z a-fightin' one mornin' said oh, man, it wuz jist as cold as it could be. He said he'z loadin' his rifle, had steel ramrods, he said when he got his rifle loaded why he jus' turned his ramrod around, tuh put it back in under his gun, had loops in under gun barrel tuh put yer ramrod in. Said when he started t' turnin' thuh ramrod aroun' why he hit Uncle with it right on the end of thuh nose. It uz rill cold an' Uncle said, "Well, by the Lord God—Dink, they've shot the end uh my nose off!" [*I laugh*]

KID: He called Grandad "Dink." Said he jus' fell over on the groun', commenced to rollin' aroun', said he let him roll aroun' a while, said he said, "Aaah," he said, "Dick, I jes' hit yuh on the end of thuh nose with muh gun rod." Uncle Dick thought he had the end of his nose shot off. Sometimes them ol' boys ud git in such a hurry t' shoot, they wouldn't take thuh ramrod out uv their gun barroll. They'd fire their gun off with them ramrods an' they'd shoot 'um plum through one uh them pretty good-size trees. Twelve-fourteen inches through—why that ol' rifle ud jes' shoot that ramrod plum through there.

JOSEPH: Then I suppose it would go right through a man.

KID: Yaah . . . But you know, Uncle Dick, Grandad said when they'd be out fightin' in the open—why, he'd try tuh stand behind yuh.

JOSEPH: No kidding . . .

One evening in the Indian summer of early fall, Kid Cougar and I sit in the old swing on the front porch of the ancient house. He tells me how the women would comb out their long hair with kerosene to kill any lice which might seek homes in their tresses. "Ah, Joseph, females wuz rill women then." A good woman, he tells me, would never expose herself publicly the way women do now, with clothing designed for the purpose, but no one raised an eyebrow when a mother breast fed a child in church during Sunday services. "Yuh never had no trouble tellin' the whores from the ladies in them days." The sun streaks through the great trees all about the house and creates a yellow-orange patchwork on the black earth and faded grass. We talk of feuds between families and clans, murders and shoot outs. Some of these passionate clashes would pass for classical tragedies, or bittersweet myths of some faraway, bygone culture. Kid binds me to secrecy concerning a number of these histories. Descendants of men who killed one another simultaneously still live in the region of Dark Hill. ". . . the bullet struck ol' Sam b'tween the eyes," as he stood in his doorway and his adversary "wuz blasted clean off his hoss" by a double-hammered shot from Sam's double-barreled twelve gauge muzzle-loading gun. The horse "took off like a shot cat" and Kid can tell me the number of shot the doctor dug from the body (only two shot missed). I hear a tragic tale of incest and the fierce feud which resulted between a young woman's brother and the girl's lover whom the brother publicly blamed for his sister's pregnancy. The squirrels come out to chatter and play now; they are not afraid. The Kid talks of God-fearing people now, people who worked hard all their lives and wronged no one. He tells me of farmers, ranchers, tradesmen and blacksmiths, and the sometimes saintly women who made the homes and sought to create a fine culture for their children. One carpenter who immigrated from the mountains of Tennessee after the Civil War, "them people always bring uh piece uh the mountains along with 'em, Joe . . . ," was the finest Christian that the Kid ever met. An old she-squirrel with no tail has lived in the oak tree which stands closest to the porch. She has inhabited the tree for well over ten years. She looks up at us from the old front brick walk that leads into the woods. The Kid now talks to me of Uncle Coon Balder. "Uncle Coon Balder use t' git drunk when he wuz jist uh young fellah an' run his hoss up an' down the wooden sidewalks in Fenton. He wuz sich a horseman the only way they cud stop 'im uz t' shoot his horse out frum under 'im. When I wuz a kid boy ah asked ol' Uncle Coon 'bout that, he sez, 'Yeah, I had two er three good uns shot out from under me!' " The old she-squirrel blends now her mad chatter with the old cowboy's soft drawl; the porch swing squeaks with its subtle groaning; the sun sets.

KID: You know some people is allergic to uh bee sting. But up to this particular time it doesn't affect me a bit in thuh world. If you let a honey bee sting yuh ever so often . . . it'll cut down thuh possibility of cancer.

JOSEPH: Any sort of cancer?

KID: Any kind uh cancer . . . I'z talkin' tuh Hazel Mason the other day. Her grandmother Mazier wore uh kin' ah uh cardboard down over her nose. She got thuh cancer. She said there wuz uh-ah we use t' call 'em trampers, bums yuh know, we called 'em trampers. She said there wuz one of them come by one day. Said he wanted uh meal. He said, "Now fer yer meal" she had this cancer of thuh nose, sez, "I wanna give you a box of salve." Sez, "It'll cure that cancer." Well, he give her the box of salve fer his meal, and by Jove she cured up her nose.

JOSEPH: Really?

KID: Yes sir.

JOSEPH: Well, many of those old remedies were developed by experience. There's no telling who that tramp was.

KID: Now say, that tramp, he wuz pretty wise.

JOSEPH: Perhaps she entertained an angel unaware.

KID: Well, you know, Joe, Christ could uv give it to her, disguised as uh tramp.

JOSEPH: Whoever does something for one of the least of these, does it for me? [*The cock crows*]

KID: Now tramps use t' be very plentiful. But they modernized thuh name an' called it "hobo."

KID: Joe, I always thought when uh child wuz raised on a bottle it inherited the disposition of the bottle. [I *laugh*]

JOSEPH: Or, the cow?

KID: An' where it's raised on the breast it inherits its mother's disposition. Now what's yore version uv that?

JOSEPH: I think common sense tells one that breast feeding is more nourishing and right for the child, assuming the mother is healthy.

KID: You take most any animal, the young nurses the mother.

Joe, I b'lieve we kin git in yonder now an' be more comfortable.

JOSEPH: All right. [*The dogs bark*]

A pot bellied stove sits in the main room of the old house; the stove pipe runs into the ancient hearth and through the flue gives up sweet-wood smoke to the winter air. Often in the evenings we sit semi-circled of the smouldering iron and talk late into the bitter cold winter nights. Under the house the dogs occasionally growl with tentative concern, for they are dreaming of the wolves. As I listen to the old men talk I hear a siren song for the old days growing in my heart and in the dim red glow of the stove which radiates heat into the dusky, lamplit atmosphere there appear to my mind's eye many things.

KID: Dad said they took this uh Jack Stone out an' throwed 'im up on thuh woodpile tuh keep thuh hogs from eatin' 'im up. Says there wuz a great big ol' long tall fat boy there, they jist took him out on thuh prairie, jist marked across his head, yuh know, an' his feet an down his sides an' scooped out a hole in that sand. That's where they left ol' Jack Stone. Jist with his clothes an' boots on, jist like he wuz pushed thuh dirt on him. Pulled thuh saddle off his horse, an' bridle, turned his horse loose. Nobody didn't know uh thing in thuh world about him a-tall. That's how tight ever body wuz. You never saw a feller there in Oklahoma without he had a rifle on the saddle, one six-shooter (on his belt) an' maybe one on his saddle. That wuz about-oh, long in thuh eighties.

There was an old log house with one window. In it was a trunk full of Confederate money. The children would play with the money and then return it to the trunk.

KID: Joe, those wild hogs 'll jist cut yuh into.

JOSEPH: They will eat your flesh, won't they?

KID: Yow, they'll eat you up, boy.

A man must be careful when shooting a wild hog in the brush. The hog's fellows may be roosting in low branches of the trees from whence they may leap out and set upon the hunter in a pack.

KID: Joe, you take watchin' a fire iz kinda like watchin' uh cloud. But you take nature iz a wonderful thing.

JOSEPH: It is.

KID: But there's so many diff'rent things that we don't understand.

JOSEPH: What kind of a school did you attend when you were a child, Kid?

KID: Jist uh country school, Joe, walked there an' walked back.

JOSEPH: What was it like?

KID: Well, sir, there wuz uh hunnerd an' seventy students an' two teachers.

JOSEPH: Two teachers?

KID: Yeah—taught all them kids. You never saw as many of thuh little devils on the school playyard in yore life.

JOSEPH: (I laugh) Did they have different rooms?

KID: They had two rooms.

JOSEPH: Two.

KID: Then later on they built three (a third room). Them teachers 'ud draw fifteen tuh twenty dollars uh month an' they'd walk tuh thuh schoolhouse an' walk back.

JOSEPH: Those school teachers were pretty strict, weren't they?

KID: Ah—they'z crusty ol' boys. They'd tear your britches up!

JOSEPH: They were men.

KID: Yeah, they were men. Some women, an' them women wuz hard-crusted ol' girls.

When Lim reached the age of sixteen he studied under a schoolmarm neither crusty nor old. She was a pretty young woman, who in later years got a degree with honors from a prestigious eastern college. She encouraged Lim's interest in poetry, and he composed these verses for her:

AUTUMN LEAVES

I.   The autumn winds are blowing,
The leaves are falling fast,
The great Snow King is coming
to cover up the mash.

II. The squirrels are seeking shelter,
In among the hollow trees,
With nuts stored up for winter,
And now they rest with ease.

III. The farmer sees no trouble,
For his crops are in the store.
Soon the great big Thanksgiving turkey
will depart for evermore.

LIM: If she'd been a little more my age, Joseph, why—ah'd shore considered somethin'. I like smart women, boy, don't you?

JOSEPH: Sure.

When the Kid was still a boy he attended a school which derived its water supply from a narrow well on the school grounds. One day the rope of the well bucket was broken and some of the pretty little girls were thirsty, so Kid took the bucket and shinnied down the well sideways by using his back and feet for support. He was about fifteen feet down, "It uz jist as black as it could be down there, Joe," when he glanced up and saw the school teacher's unfriendly face frowning down from within the circle of light at the top. That was the day that Kid Cougar first began to gain a public reputation for being spontaneously reckless. When he was a grown man and riding down an outlaw horse, an observer remarked to his father: "S'i," (says I) "Mr. ———, you only raised one boy. That one's too wild. He couldn' uh been raised!"

LIM: The Kid did some daredevil things all thuh time he wuz young. (By "daredevil things" Lim does not refer to planned stunts, but, rather, wild spur of moment recklessness, often involving wild animals or gunplay.)

KID: Ah, Joe, I don't see how I ever got growed.

We talk of the Kid's all-time favorite horse, a bay whose name was Dan.

KID: Them ol' buggy horses like ol' Dan, they's uh unusual type horse, but you couldn't—aw, you could handle him quiet plowin' with uh double-shovel, plowin' thuh orchards . . . first time we plowed we plow up an' down thuh hill. Second time we'd plow crossways the hill, yuh know, to keep it from washin'.

JOSEPH: Yes.

KID: But that ol' boy when you's a-workin' him, why the first time yuh went aroun' in thuh trees he always watch the trees an' smell to see if thuh's wasp nest in 'em. If thuh's wasp nest in 'em he'd shy around 'em. (The trees were set out in a checkered pattern.) But he's wise in uh way, in other ways I thought he's jist uh—dumb.

JOSEPH: Dan was high-strung?

KID: Uh-huh. But you could holler a time er two he'd be doin' fine—you could holler at him a time er two—man he'd jist go wild, didn't have a bit a sense a-tall. (Kid used Dan for everything except working cattle. He used an "ol' black stag horse" which was much more settled for cow work.)

JOSEPH: Dan was a good travelling horse, wasn't he?

KID: Yow, he'z uh runnin' horse. He'd outrun a Model-T Ford. But one 'ud pass yuh runn'n wide open, you could kick him out he'd get his strut in forty er fifty yards. But he jumped twenty foot the first jump he made.

JOSEPH: No kidding.

KID: But he'd jist sprang—God boy he'd hit thuh ground runnin'.

Of all the home-bred horses and mules only old Skeet is left. The dark horse-mule is now in his middle thirties. Benignly serene, he shadows Kid Cougar about the pastures. His dwelling place is the north barn, which he enters and leaves at will. Kid also tells me of the bucking horse of his prime, which horse, says the Kid, did not require a pinch strap.

JOSEPH: Dan enjoyed running, didn't he?

KID: He liked to run. Yah-boy he could git up an' get gone!

When Kid went to a social function with his fiddle (Nicholas Amatus), he rode Dan. He also rode Dan to rodeos, and old Uncle Coon Balder would saddle up and ride along.

KID: Uncle Coon he talked through his nose. (Kid talks through his nose when he quotes Uncle Coon.) "By God if yuh go t'uh rodeo, come by I wanna go with yuh." He ride an' old cat-trottin' horse . . .

JOSEPH: Cat-trotting?

KID: Yow—jist ol' straight trottin' mare, I'd say "Can yer horse fox-trot Uncle Coon?" "No, by God, but she's got uh good cowtrot!" (I laugh.) He'd set up on that old horse, an' she'd jest hit the ground stiff legged, yuh know, jes' bump, bump, bump . . . He wore uh big four Stetson hat an' he never crushed the top. Said when you 'uz out in a rain storm said they wouldn't turn the "worter." But we'd ride along, he'd tell me uh diff'rent things happened along uh road an' various places in sight.

The old cowboys have a family history that is truly American: They live in the middle of a section of land in a house that was built in 1857. Kid was a cowboy, bronc-buster, a blacksmith, a wild-west show rider, and an early day rodeo cowboy. Lim was a cowboy, an old-style ladies' man, and a dancer who danced throughout the country towns of Texas. With their father they ranched and raised high cotton in the days when horse power was literal. Two great-grandfathers fought in the Texas Revolution; their paternal grandfather and his four brothers fought for the Confederacy; their father roamed Indian Territory as a cowboy and an adventurer. They are most proud, however, of their Indian blood. Their paternal grandmother was a beautiful Comanche who could sit upon her hair. Kid and Lim believe that of all the people in the world, the American Indian has a right to complain bitterly and to hate. Kid tells me that the Plains Indian could never have been defeated except for the destruction of their natural economy in the slaughter of the buffalo. European diseases, too, killed many, he says. "Joseph, them warriors—I mean they wuz all man!" Lim says that people with Indian blood are different from all others. "We's queer-streaked, Joe boy."

Lim Hang High danced many steps. In his best dance he used a hat. One night he danced before about four thousand people in a public building. Halfway through the difficult hat dance Lim dropped the hat, but he improvised and incorporated into his dance the dropping of the hat and its retrieval. When Lim finished that dance, says Kid, one would have thought the roof of the building would rise up airborne from the force of the applause.

The old stove is cooling as the cock crows again. The barns are empty except for the ghost horses that are gone, while Kid Cougar rides old Dan every night in his dreams. Lim is stove-up in one leg and the Kid knows in his heart that time is taking its dues. The dusty used-up old calendars hang in semidarkness. The two old cowboys who have refused to worship the vile modern gods "they say" and "we now know" wait patiently for the High-Man to call. But even as they wait for the end, they love their life and their black land.

JOSEPH: Kid, how is old Skeet?

KID: Ah, Joseph, ol' Skeet is dead. He jes' laid down an' died out in thuh north barn.

JOSEPH: Ah . . .

KID: Well, Joe, let's uh fill up the egg carton, un git it somewhere where you won't go off an' fergit it. But tuh heck, I'm awful forgetful, my mind comes an' goes—left me when I wuz uh kid an' never has come back yet. [*Mutual laughter*]

JOSEPH: Well, at least you know it's somewhere. [*The cock crows*] Lim, are you going to read us that poem now?

LIM: Here is one that I composed the sixth night of February, 1965. This is an old home, country home. I thought of all thuh people that I visited 'n that old home. Walkin' up the old walk, I wuz inspired by these words:

A home that is silent
A path untrod
A voice is still
A song is unsung
A web is unbroken
A life is done
A sweet journey into
A life beyond.

JOSEPH: That's good, Lim. Is that the last one you've written?
[*Lim nods yes*]

JOSEPH: Did you tell me it was a stormy night?

LIM: Stormy night . . . it wuz uh stormy night and I wuz all alone . . . sixth night of February, Saturday night, 1965. I have a habit when I'm alone an' my mind goes clickin'. An' I can think better, act better—an' I hope I look better too when I'm in that state of mind (chuckles softly). You want me to relate some uh them dance steps I wuz tellin' you about?

JOSEPH: Sure.

LIM: Well you know I told you before, Joe boy, that I danced thirty-five perfected dance steps. I can recite quite a few uv 'em now at the present time. My brother rode Wild West sixteen year. He wuz (a) professional rider. He said when he got up there to ride, he got up there to ride! He didn't git up there like a lot of the present-day riders do. Get on and get off. But he got up there to ride. They used to put the money on him. They'd run aroun' and say, "Kid, I've got so much money on you. You let that bronc throw yuh, I'll split thuh deal with yuh." Said, "Listen here! I don't do that kind uh stuff. When I get up there tuh ride, a'hm damn sure gonna ride!"

KID: I rode tuh stay on top.

LIM: He went thuh rough an' rugged way, thuh bronc-bustin'.

An' I took the easy side of it. I played vaudahville. I perfected thirty-five diff'rent dance steps. I remember quite a few
of thuh steps. I remember quite a few uv thuh steps that
I started off on:

> Sit to cut thuh buckle
> Chikin plucker set-to
> Side shuffle
> Hen wallet west
> Grapevine twist
> Walkin' up thuh trail
> Showin' how thuh colored folks walk when they went out
>   to get thuh white folks chickin
> An' dancin' up thuh steps an' down thuh steps

An' I never lost a note in the performance. I'm far re-
moved from the former situation. But thuh good Lord's a-
helpin' me an' I hope to regain my physical strength and
composure again. If thuh High-Man is willin'. I also danced
the double-shuffle an' professional hoe-down.

Boy, I'm ugly, ugly as can be, but I wish tuh be good to
everything livin'. But now the Kid there, he's in uh diff'rent
class. All thuh girls—they want the Kid. But when they look
at me—why they make a face! [*Laughter*] I admire the Kid's
manhood highly. I lord him like no one else ever done uh
brother.

In the early spring the Kid and I feed the cattle at the north
barn. We climb into the loft and kick out several big bales of
Johnson. Then we sit in the loft opening, dangling our legs,
and Kid Cougar calls his cattle in from the pasture and up from
the creek bottoms. "Ho! heah cows! Ho! Ho! Heah cow!" One
cow appears, then two, three, six, "Ho cow!" twelve, fifteen,
"Heah cow! Ho!" While the herd of about fifty come together
below us, occasionally lowing and mooing, the old cowboy frets
over each as if it were his child. "That white-face hadn't dropped

yet, Joe—ah, that motley one iz goin' back fer her calf." We discuss the new calves whose faces are still white as snow and the Kid wonders rhetorically, "How do you reken their mammies tell them apart, boy, they all look jest the same?" We discuss their lowing, wondering if they communicate the same as people. These are topical questions to the Kid, but he keeps the answers to himself, preferring to test my knowledge. His eyes narrow like an old chief in council when I reply, but he treasures his secrets in his heart. I can tell, however, that he believes that the cattle do indeed have a language like people, for he has heard them speak to one another since his birth, ". . . when the world wuz pretty young." Now we go down among the cattle. We spread out the hay, gather up the baling wire, and consider the merits of the two bulls. On our way back to the house Kid Cougar digs up an Indian turnip for me and admonishes me severely, "Now don't you never eat one uh these, Joe boy, they'll shore burn like thuh dickens."

In the summer we sit at the table in the dining room and eat ice cream. Through the screen door I can see the hounds lying on the L-shaped side porch. The dogs here are happy dogs. Sometimes at night when the wolves come in close, the dogs howl all together in eerie harmony. The summer in this country is hot, and a man feels lazy in the cool shaded house, watching the hounds pant and stretch, and listening to the grasshoppers in the dry brush. The Kid says, "Take off yer shirt, Joe . . . make yerself at home." Lim smiles and says, "Joe boy, try some uh this soda pop on that ice cream. It shore iz good, boy." These old men have a subtle feeling for enjoying life.

LIM HANG HIGH: (singing)

> Old Missus Johnson got troubles of her own
> She's got an old yellah cat that won't stay at home
> She give him to a farmer tha's a-movin' out west
> The very next day the cat come back.

Cat come back
Cat come back
He wouldn't stay away

[*Stomps severely in time*]

Old Missus Johnson lives all alone
In an old pine cottage she can call her own
Where the old cat come and the cat went
The old cat come but he just couldn't quit.

Cat come back
Cat come back
Couldn't stay away

JOSEPH: That's good, Lim! [*I clap*]
LIM: Thank yuh, Joe . . .
    I give out quick. I just got suh hot! [*Laughs*]
JOSEPH: That's good. That's got a lot of style.
LIM: I practice it a whole lot. I practice that stuff yuh know
    when I'm out. Sometimes I have better voice for a rendition
    than I had that time. I don't . . . how does my voice sound?
JOSEPH: Sounds pretty good to me.
LIM: The Kid's voice sounds good. He has a kind of uh . . .
    Uncle George Weatherby voice.
    The Kid has come in with chunks of wood for the fire. He
puts these in the pot-bellied stove. He says:
KID: Ah—if we could play (music) like we used to, Joe . . .
    There's a man out here yesterdy with his boy. I replaited a
    whup fer his boy . . . a stock whup, a six-plait, an' let's see,
    I plaited a lariat fer 'em.
KID: I usetah pick four hunnerd pounds of cotton uh day, Joe.
JOSEPH: That's a lot of cotton, a lot of bending over, isn't it?
KID: But I did most of my pickin' crawlin'.
JOSEPH: Crawling?
KID: Yeh, ah crawled. I usetah pick with Bill Hooper. He picked
    with me when he wuz an ol' kid boy 'bout fourteen yers old.

He'd jus' stay close enough to me tuh hear my sack draggin'
. . . me an' him 'ud pick a little over eight hunnerd pounds
uh day, four hunnerd uh piece. But it didn't seem to me like
I'z workin' hard. But I jus' kept steady at it. But he'd beat
me two er three pound ever way an' he stayed behind me all
thuh time. I guess he got more dirt in his.

JOSEPH: Yes . . . you crawled?

KID: Yeah, ah'd crawl.

JOSEPH: On all fours?

KID: No, I'd jes' crawl on muh knees, you see. Stand up on
mah knees and crawl along on muh knees.

JOSEPH: Oh, walk on your knees. Did it make your knees sore?

KID: I told yuh about pullin' cotton on crutches.

JOSEPH: After that mare fell on you?

KID: Yeah. But you know a bad bruise, Joe, is worse'n uh break.

JOSEPH: Is it?

KID: It shore is. You get over it slower.

JOSEPH: I broke my hand working with a horse last spring.
When I do heavy work, it aches in a pronounced manner.

KID: As yuh get older it'll get worse.

JOSEPH: Really?

KID: Uh-huh. But I had both mah arms broke, mah leg, mah
nose, mah ribs . . .

JOSEPH: Do they ache?

KID: Well, sometimes ah hurt suh bad all over I can't tell where
ah hurt the worse.

JOSEPH: I guess it's normal then. I won't be concerned about it.

KID: We usetah tuh be awful bad to bird hunt, Joe. If it uz
rainin' bad, snow on the ground we'd all go bird huntin'
(game birds). One time we'z down in the creek here huntin'
and there uz a big snow on the ground tha'z thawed.

JOSEPH: Yes?

KID: Yuh know when the snow begins to thaw er ice the water'll
be movin'.

JOSEPH: Right.

KID: An' the creek wuz up aroun' half bank full. It wuz cold,
cold as the dickens. But the birds come up an flew across the

creek. I smoke a pipe then all the time. Dad sez, "You boys climb one of them willow trees, bend yuh across the creek." Sez: "I'll fetch up a gun," sez, "unloaded." All right. Well I crawled up the tree first, and I jus' swung in under it. Got it far enough I figured it 'ud land us on the other bank.

JOSEPH: Yes . . .

KID: Ol' Lem, he got right up over us, right up over me . . . and I uz just a-smokin' a pipe.

JOSEPH: Yes . . .

KID: He got right up over me an' we got tuh springin' that tree. It snapped off 'bout fifteen foot from thuh ground. An' we come right down in thuh center of thuh creek. An' when I come down why he hit me in thuh back uh mah head with his feet. An' I know he stuck muh head in thuh mud, cause uh, had mud in mah hair when I come up. [*I laugh*]

KID: Well, I never did see mah pipe anymore.

JOSEPH: How deep was the water, Kid?

KID: Ah, it's about six er seven foot deep. We went on down to the old store. The old fellah that run thuh store built up uh good fire in thuh stove, got it hot. We got to settin' around thuh stove; thuh longer we set there the cooler we got. Lim says, "We better go back home an' get these wet clothes off." Sez, "Might make us sick." Guess better do that. Well we took off, we had to walk 'bout two an' uh half miles up thuh creek here.

JOSEPH: Yes . . .

KID: We took off up here an' changed clothes. But that ruined our huntin' fer thuh day. We never did go huntin' agin (that day).

One day in early summer Kid, Lim, and I visit the waterfall in the woods. Lim sits down at the edge of the creek's clearing on a fallen tree and meditates with clear eyes. Kid and I sit down reclining at the ledge's edge and watch the water descend into the dark pool. One thing about these men which impresses me strongly is their cultured manner. Neither fits in any way the crude "redneck" stereotype of current manufactured popular lore. Their dialect is pure and unfailingly consistent in its softly enunciated semantic patterns; it is not the bastardized, postured form of Hollywood and drugstore novels. Their personalities do not contain any element of that suburban, beer drinking, western styled exaggeration which seems to represent to the public today the curious state of being "countrified." It occurs to me now that these old cowboys are to the popular stereotype thereof what the music of Jimmie Rodgers is to the popular "country" music today. When a civilization begins to degenerate it begins to parody tradition; it manufactures cheap, self-conscious forms, loud things, which badly imitate pure socially evolved forms of high cultural consciousness. In other words, these cultural lead pennies to which I refer are not only lead, but the image on them of Lincoln's head is distorted. Listen to an original recording of "The Soldier's Sweetheart" and compare it with the newer popular vein of "country" music; the difference is obvious.

A dead armadillo stares at us from the opposite bank and a black snake rests down in the pool at the water's rushing edge. I ask the Kid about the gunfighters of legend. He tells me in effect that there were many "gunmen" and few "gunfighters." But the few top men of the deadly profession were every bit as proficient as the myth. "Joseph, if you wuz to shoot one them boys from ambush an' give 'em uh death wound, they 'ud kill yuh before they hit thuh ground." We discuss gun fights in general and I learn that men really did meet at noon or sundown, men who were just average with a pistol. "They'd shoot each other 'til they'z out of shots, an' then some friend 'ud drag 'em off." Sometimes these western duelists lived after having five or six pieces of lead dug out of their bodies. Kid tells me that there were ambushes, however, and occasionally innocent, disinterested people blundered into these traps. Also, men often relied on each other's help in dealing with such lawless dangers. When one man was trying to mount a nervous horse in an explosive situation he called to his already mounted companion, "Don't leave me, now, don't leave me."

From the histories Kid relates it is evident that the non-gunman rancher or farmer usually chose a double barreled shotgun when faced with an attack by a gunman; often the rancher would wait for the attacking gunman to get in range, then leap out from behind his door or a concealing tree (depending on his relative location) and trust his luck to the pull of both triggers.

On our way back through the woods which are browning now in the heat, Lim points out the largest cottonwood tree I have ever seen. He was using it for a sapling walking stick and subsequently planted it here, when he was seventeen. Lim loves and reveres trees deeply, and I can see a gentle light in his eyes when he contemplates the sacred cottonwoods and straight pines. These trees are to him what Mozart's horn concertos are to some music lovers, and, indeed, I think Lim's personality reminds me of Mozart's concertos. He is such an engagingly open balance; noble, lightly forceful, and in no way pompous.

LIM: White Bull was the nephew of Sitting Bull. He's thuh last great chieftain that kept a record of thuh Indian's history uv their time. Kept uh history. Kept it on a elk hide. He wuz the last one of thuh chiefs that could read them ol' . . . them ol' histories, Indian histories.

KID: Kind uv uh rebus.

LIM: And it wuz recorded from one winter to another. Wuz accurate too. Them Indians even kept account of the Civil War and them famous battles.

KID: They'd mark time one moon to another, and from one winter to another. So many moons, so many winters.

KID: Joe, you don't wanta fish in uh light moon, tha's light night. You wanna fish in dark moon. The catfish, they go back under thuh log, under holes in thuh bank, under drifts in uh light moon. They don't come out. But in uh dark moon why yunno he'll come out an' feed.

LIM: Indians understood the moon phases better than any other tribe uv people anywhere.

KID: Lots of people don't think thuh moon has anything to do with thuh weather conditions. Now you know it has all in the world to do with thuh weather conditions.

JOSEPH: It certainly affects the tides.

KID: Now if we start havin' moon changes in the evenin', Joe, it turn off dry. As long as we have our moon changes in the mornin' she'll go tuh rainin' and showrin', we gonna have bad weather. But when that moon goes tuh changin' in thuh evenin', in thuh evenin' about four o'clock, why rain's over. Lots uh people laugh at yuh, yuh tell 'em anything about thuh moon.

JOSEPH: Yes.

KID: Now when yuh plant anything that has all in thuh world whatever you're plannin' on producin'.

JOSEPH: Yes.

KID: But you take anythin' in thuh way uv uh vine that blooms, melon vine, tomato vine, an' sech as that, you uh plant them seeds or set 'em out when thuh signs in thuh bloom, they won't never produce anything. They'll jist bloom like nobody's business. But they won't have any fruit on them a-tall. You take cucumbers—why thuh vines'll grow suh fast they'll drag thuh little cucumbers off thuh vine. But they won't never mature. Lot uh people just scoff at you, if you plant anything in thuh sign. But I suppose if yuh plantin' melons or anythin' like that, if the sign was in thuh head, they'd grow large and round. But don't never plant or put out any vine or anything that bears fruit when the signs in thuh privates. They'll bloom but boy she won't produce. Yuh take tomato vines, bean vines, melon vines, cucumber vines, they'll jist bloom themselves tuh death.

JOSEPH: Both of you profess the Christian religion, right?

KID: Uhuh, we both believe in thuh golden rule.

LIM: Yes sir!

JOSEPH: I wanted that for the record.

KID: The Bible says, "Cast your bread upon the water an' after many days it shall return to thee."

LIM: Christ said, "Do unto others as you would have them do unto you."

JOSEPH: Right . . .

LIM: Christ said, "As I have been unto you likewise so will I
be agin, for lo I am with thee always." Who'z he a-talkin' to?
He uz a-talkin' to them that confess't Him. He uz a-talkin'
to them that sought and found Him. He'z a-talkin' to them
that believed an' pressed Him. He is not talkin' to them that
cain't understand, won't understand. They—they don't know
Him. They won't try to get acquainted with Him. He is a-
talkin' an' promisin' them that has confessed theirself unto
His great and Holy name, the Lord Jesus Christ. How well
it tis to remember these famous words, spoken by one of
our great American poets, when he said, "An' this way we
walk but one time. We are here today and with God's
promise to witness the downing of tomorrow."

KID: Rekon we ought tuh have uh song? [*Mutual laughter*]

KID: Well, it's nuthin' tuh laugh about boys: Because we all
come here without our consent an' we leave the very same
way.

JOSEPH: That's true.

KID: An' we don't take a thing in the world but what they put on
us. But you know, Joe, you'd be just as well in uh pine box
buried in the fence row or out in the center of a field,
than you would with all thuh clothes that they can put on
yuh an keep your grave up with flowers. That don't help you
a bit. If you've got any flowers tuh strow, strow 'em while the
individual is livin'. Don't wait 'till after he's dead then heap
flowers on his grave, because he cain't see 'em.

JOSEPH: That's good, Kid. You boys have a fine way of ex-
pressing yourselves.

KID: You boys talk, I've got tuh see about something.

LIM: I study the Scriptures a lot. I'm serious-minded. An' when
I get off by myself, I get right down tuh business.

KID: I'll tell you Joe if yuh ever lose a front tooth—it'll impair
yore speech boy. Yuh talk like yuh're toungue-tied.

LIM: Christ Jesus, Our Lord and Our God in Heaven. We
thank Thee Master Our Father Our God for this wonderful
privilege, that Thou has suffered us to be together in a great

endeavor for humanity and whosoever will select this writin'
in behalf of we who hast labored all of our lives for a
better way of life for the coming generations. Help us, Lord.
Keep us forever in thy great keepin'. Sustain us, Master . . .
for a great way and a wonderful life . . . more so here and
in the greater hereafter. We ask thee, Master, to remember
all, all we've ever tried to remember for thuh wonderful askin'.
Please forgive us, Lord. Please, deliver us from death. Keep us,
Master, forever in thy great keepin'. We pray Thee.

In Christ Jesus Name,
Amen.

One afternoon I watch Kid put the chickens to bed. The hen
coop is divided into halves with a separate door for both
sections. Kid opens the door on one side and says, "Let's go tuh
bed, come on." About half the chickens proceed without hesitation
to enter that side of the coop and then the process is repeated,
with most of the remaining chickens entering the other section on
the cowboy's command. Five mavericks fly to their usual roosts in
trees and now we go feed the dogs. One of the dogs is a great
hound named Ol' Trail. When it is dark, his eyes glow red,
and he has jaws like an alligator. I am glad that I knew him
when he was a pup. Trail was given to a horse-rancher friend
three times when he was half-grown and three times he found
his way back across country to the tree-shrouded pine home.
This place is dog heaven on the seventh level, and this collection
of hounds, curs, and half-wolf mongrels know it well.

The old cowboy sits down on the back side porch, and I
lean against the adjacent well and we talk of the world today,
the world which these men do not know and do not care to meet.
Except for an occasional visit with old friends in one of the nearby
tiny towns and the journalism of the farm quarterly, Kid and
Lim live in peaceful isolation. They prefer this isolation, for their
world has passed away and left them alone with memories.
Some of their memories are of gentle matters, and some are of
the lusty and fierce things of bygone days. I tell Kid Cougar

that some people in this country have actually begun eating horse meat and feel no sense of shame over it. All the time that I have known Kid Cougar he has never raised his voice. To make verbal emphasis, he simply varies the shading of his soft, low drawl. But now, at hearing of this abomination, his eyes light up with fire, and his right hand in a reflex action reaches for the absent .45 thumb-buster that no longer hangs on his thigh, and he raises his voice and his accent becomes vehement, "Joe, I think people that eats horses is going to hell!" I tell him that I think eating horses is the last thing to do before starving and that he has a good point. His manner softens some and the fire in his eyes becomes pain and he says, "But heckfire, Joseph, horses is just good people." "Kid, some of my best friends are horses," say I, as Ol' Trail lies down on the porch and pants, showing his great teeth. I have seen today across the many years and for an instant stood face to face with the Kid Cougar that brave men didn't cross.

KID: Joe, the last kid I saw breast fed wuz by uh preacher's wife. She started her baby out on thuh breast and in about six weeks—two months jist cut off an' put it on thuh bottle.

JOSEPH: How old were you when you were weaned, Kid?

KID: Two an' uh half. But you know Joe, sometimes uh woman's milk ud sour.

JOSEPH: The world has changed a great deal since you were a child, hasn't it, Kid?

KID: Say boy, it's jist as much a daylight an' dark.

JOSEPH: Would you care to elaborate some on that?

KID: Joe, we'd go tuh uh picnic back then, there wuzn't any kind uh motor vehicle a-tall. It uz all wagons, buggies, horseback an' afoot. They uz as many there afoot as there wuz in vehicles there. They'd start tuh breakin' up, some uh them ol' horses spooky an' they'd booger an' run away with uh buggy an' tear it all tuh pieces. I remember an' ol' horse named Molly spookin' at somethin' an' when they found her the next day all she had on wuz thuh collar.

KID: I reckon Joe mah eyes gets in uh 'clipse ever once in awhile. I'll get to lookin' fer anything . . . I jus' can't see it atall. I rekon that's what's wrong with uh feller—his eyes gets in uh 'clipse.

JOSEPH: Well, when you get used to seeing something, you look at it and you don't see it. It doesn't register. That was Corky out there with a litter, wasn't it?

KID: Uh-huh.

JOSEPH: I think she has a litter every time I look around. [*The dogs bark*]

KID: She is very prolific, Joe; she is very fertil . . . Well, I've got to go get me some matches, boys, come in here and fergotten 'em.

LIM: Matches? Here's uh book. [*Kid goes out*] Ol' Kid keeps them smokes goin'. Shore to pull them cigarettes. You won't never start anything like that—you won't have tuh stop it. Young people oughtah be very careful about what they start.

JOSEPH: Right.

LIM: Our mother—ah she wuz just as tight on me an' Kid as we been girls. She shore wuz exactin'. She wuz uh good-lookin' woman an' she wuz smart.

JOSEPH: Smart?

LIM: Ah-smart! She wuz a walkin' encyclopedia.

JOSEPH: No kidding.

LIM: If yuh told her anything, she never forgot it. You could see her ten years after yuh met her an' she could tell you ever word of thuh conversation that you an' her had spoke to one another. I b'lieve she had the most remarkable memory, Joe, not cause she uz our mother, of any person I ever saw. She had a memory jes' like an elephant.

JOSEPH: Total recall?

LIM: She could tell you thuh first word that they ever give out the door save thuh first day she went to school, spring classes. She knew ever poem. She could recite poetry to you all day, set up that night an' never say the same one twice. An' she wrote poetry. An' she composed genuine poetry. Tha's where I inherited my ability for such things as that.

JOSEPH: Do you have any of her poetry left?

LIM: Yes, there's some here.

JOSEPH: I wish you'd dig it out sometime and read it for me.

LIM: I'm gonna do that; I'm gonna do that. But ever day, me and Kid have tuh do something—like cut wood. If she ever called me to her bedside. You know she wuzn't active. She couldn't set up.

KID: Well, she'z an invalid (in her last years).

LIM: Whenever she called me up to her I knew I had somethin' comin.' I get my paper an' pencil and write her down.

JOSEPH: Really? [*The dog barks*]

LIM: She called me one day an' tol' me, sez there's three answers to prayer. Yes, no, and maybe. Christ said, "Come unto me an' I will give you rest." And he also said, "No, ye are not of my sheep." Now he wuz a-talkin' to them that couldn't understand. They wouldn't understand. They couldn't believe. They wudn't a-gonna believe. Christ also said, "Wait, I have somethin' better for you." I wrote all that down. [*A dog barks fiercely under the house*] An the minister used 'em when he preached her funeral. An' it astonished thuh congregation. Never heard it before. They jus' looked at one another. She had the nicest funeral you ever went to.

KID: But they preached her funeral in thuh Christian Church. Preached Dad's funeral in thuh Baptist Church. But Dad— he had uh large funeral.

LIM: I got tuh hunt that poem that she wrote. The first line she first started it off. Sez, "The rich spoils of memories are mine." Now we're gonna put that line on her headstone. We've got tuh buy her uh headstone, boy. We put it off all thuh time.

KID: Dad hadn't been away jest a little bit 'fore we put a headstone up, his grave.

LIM: She'd say things you never here'd uv before. Dad would too, before he passed away. He said some things—I wish I'd a-wrote that down. But I'll never think of it in thuh world.

You know about thuh afterlife. What we've got a-comin'. Yuh think we can understand that an' we try to visualize in our minds how that ud be. But we can't—we can't, we can't. We can't compare our life with thuh one to come. If we accept the Lord Jesus Christ as our Savior. An' you've done that, an' we all have.

KID: I tell yuh, fellas. Most all preachers—they'll preach anything jus' like they understand it. An' there's very few them that preaches exactly alike.

JOSEPH: Yes, that's true.

KID: But jes' keep thuh ten commandments . . .
Well, thuh dumplin' is a-trompin' up an' down in thuh pan. They're gonna be hot d'rectly. But we'll have to do like we do thuh coffee—saucer it an' blow it.

One day, a short time ago, Kid Cougar went to a small country store to purchase some dry cereal dog food for his hounds and curs. At the store some young people approached him and began to preach to him. Cougar listened politely and gently thanked the youths for their concern for his soul. Later he told me that they warned him to "beware of the bark of the beast."

KID: Joseph, what do you rekon them young-uns meant by that, "beware of the bark of the beast?"

JOSEPH: Kid, either you misunderstood their modern English enunciation, and they actually said, "mark of the beast," or you understood them properly and they meant for you to beware of television. But since you have no electricity (kerosene lamps and wood-burning stoves) you are quite safe.

I brought a transistor radio for Kid Cougar but he won't listen to any of the music and the news simply confirms him in his opinion that the world went mad sometime ago. He listens to baseball games, though.

Cougar's favorite joke concerns a turn-of-the-century bum who was trying to convince a farm matron that he was a Christian. (She gave handouts to Christians.) He had been schooled by another bum to say that his favorite part of the Bible was the story about Samson in which Samson took the jawbone of an ass and slew a thousand Philistines. Sadly, he got mixed up while being interrogated by the farm woman and said that he liked Samson because Samson had beaten the ass off a thousand Philistines with a jawbone.

Kid speaks deprecatingly of John Wesley Hardin and says that Wyatt Earp was an early-day gangster, but Ben Johnson, drunken John Ringo and the legendary Hickock were the real thing. Belle Starr, he says, was actually very foul, and Bill Longley would kill without reason.

Kid says some people claim that he was mean when he was young, but that he was never mean, only "hard-twisted."

Lim Hang High advised me never to marry or join the U.S. Army. Either way, he says, you're going to get regimented.

Lim says that once he was speaking to a young woman who passed as a lady. They were standing by a fence conversing, and once in a while she would give out a silly giggle. He looked down and saw two boys about twelve years of age reaching through the fence and up under her dress. Beware, he says, of superficial appearance. When I was five, my grandfather told me much the same thing. He said to me, "Joe, always look behind the trees."

I see an ancient photograph with yellowed edges. In it a pretty young woman sits on a grassy slope. Her brown hair is light and wispy about her face which is lit by the bright sun. She holds her closed knees with her hands and smiles.

KID: Ah, Joe, it's been uh good many moons ago.

JOSEPH: Yes.

The sun is warm. The greyness of early winter gives a curious subdued beauty to the trees and the pastures. Lim Hang High is telling me about the ants. We kneel beneath the leafless limb of a grey oak tree and examine the hole which leads to the winter chambers of the insects. "Joseph, early ever mornin' I've been a-watchin' these ants dig down in th' groun'. You know they're the world's greatest engineers. I'm a-writin' uh poem on thuh ants; one on thuh grasshoppers too. I've been studyin' them fer years." Lim often puts out sugar and molasses for the ants and watches while they take his gift into the earth. We talk of insects and birds. He tells me that the "White Man" cuts down the trees and orphans the birds. "Then these farmers get all kinds uv insecticides to kill these little bugs. Why if they'd just leave thuh brush an' trees for the birds, thuh birds ud take care uh these bugs. If a white man come up on uh beautiful flower in thuh wilderness thuh good Lord made to be beautiful, he just tromps it down. We appreciate thuh flowers, that's what thuh good Lord made us for."

"To appreciate his work?"

"Yes. You know some people say they never killed anything in their life. Why you know how many of these little insects an' ants they've killed when they've walked aroun'."

"Yes." Lim makes Indian signs in the dirt for me and he tells me of his prayer. A large grasshopper hovers in the air near Lim's ear as he speaks.

"We pray to the goodness of God
that He let us live a little longer
that we can do good every day He holds us together,
    that He lets us live.

We promise Him that we will do better ever day
    that He lets us live."

Kid Cougar appears from the field. The sun is going down, and the air begins to chill. It's time for dinner now and Kid says, "Sometimes ah git so hungry the soles of mah boots go to curlin' up an' I kin jes' reach down an' grab thuh skin uv muh stomach with muh teeth!" We all laugh and, as we climb up the steps of the old porch in order to enter the ancient house, the Kid admonishes me, "Ol' John Harker wuz uh good bad man. He shot a feller one time an' thuh bullet went in his jaw an' come out back here" (he gestures toward his posterior lobe). "Some folks'll tell yuh ol' John wuz jest uh bad man, but that's just uh hoax, Joe boy."

"Oh?" I say as we enter the door and Kid grins and says, "Boys I'm jus' like the ol' cow's tail. I'm alwuz behind."

It is in the late night that I leave my two friends. The dogs know me now and do not bark or growl as I step out on the long side porch. It is cool and fresh and the sky is purple black and the stars shine whitely like hot crystals. The storybooks of my childhood painted skies like this. The moon hides and the darkness near the earth is as dark as utter black. Kid Cougar bids me 'bye on the porch. He says that I'm one of the family now and must come back soon. "You come back an' stay with us, Joe. We'll tell people you're our younger brother." Lim sees me to my truck with the aid of an ancient kerosene lantern. He says "fare thee well, Joseph," and I tell him to take care. As I drive down the rutted dirt I look back, and I see the old man's figure silhouetted half in light, half in darkness. Then I go round the bend and the trees keep their secret to themselves once again. Presently, I recall the song verse: "Lord, I'm goin' where the water drinks like cherry wine," and like clear blue water in my mind flow these memories.

Song of the Grasshoppers

Gadabouts, and gadabout come
and gadabouts go
it's a pleasureful life
to live and to know.

Green blades to chew,
sweet blossoms to suck
when good and full
fall in the dust;
there to waller, skip,
romp and play
in the hot summer sun
the live long day.

When tired of play
rise to a height
treading the air
and casting about
for enemies that lurk
and birds of prey;
then under a sun flower
and a leaf to hide
whilst waiting for all to change
and pass me by.

But not as the ant—
I worry not
about what to do

or casting my lot;
but happy to hide
and stay away
in the last warm day
of my summer.

—LIM HANG HIGH

Have you not known? Have you not heard?
Has it not been told you from the beginning?
Have you not understood from the foundations of the
earth?

It is he who sits above the circle of the earth,
and its inhabitants are like grasshoppers;
who stretches out the heavens like a curtain,
and spreads them like a tent to dwell in;

who brings princes to nought,
and makes the rulers of the earth as nothing.

Isaiah 40:21-23